D0170383

Statue outside the convent at Rue du Bac of Our Lady speaking with Saint Catherine Labouré. Saint Catherine relates that she knelt so close to Our Lady that she rested her forearms on her knees.

ARMANDO ALEXANDRE DOS SANTOS

The Story
of the
Miraculous
Medal

A helping hand from Heaven

AMERICA NEEDS FATIMA
P.O. Box 341, Hanover, PA 17331
(888) 317-5571
ANF@ANF.org • www.ANF.org

To order additional copies of this book, please contact:

U.S.A. *$5.00*
America Needs Fatima
P.O. Box 341, Hanover, PA 17331
(888) 317-5571
ANF@ANF.org • www.ANF.org

Canada *FREE*
Canada Needs Our Lady
P.O. Box 36040, Greenfield Park, QC J4V 3N7
1-844-729-6279 (1-844-Say-Mary)
www.CanadaNeedsOurLady.org
Info@CanadaNeedsOurLady.org

Translation from Portuguese: Philip Moran
Design: Felipe Barandiarán
Cover: Elizabeth Saracino

Copyright © 2017 The American Society for the Defense of Tradition, Family and Property®—TFP®

All rights reserved. No part of this publication may be reproduced, stored in a retrieval system, or transmitted, in any form or by any means, electronic or mechanical, including photocopying, recording or any information storage and retrieval system, without prior written permission from The American Society for the Defense of Tradition, Family and Property®—TFP®.

The American Society for the Defense of Tradition, Family and Property® and TFP® are registered names of the Foundation for a Christian Civilization, Inc., a 501(c)(3) tax-exempt organization. The America Needs Fatima Campaign is a special project of the American Society for the Defense of Tradition, Family and Property®.

ISBN: 978-1-877905-40-7
Library of Congress Control Number: 2017954095
Printed in the United States of America

CONTENTS

PART I

The Miraculous Medal:
Its History and Meaning

Statue of Our Lady of Graces over the main altar in the chapel of the apparitions at Rue du Bac in Paris.

The most widespread medal of all time

The medal of Our Lady of Graces, more commonly known as the Miraculous Medal, is undoubtedly the most widespread medal of all times. It originated in France in 1830, having been revealed directly by Our Lady to Saint Catherine Labouré while yet a young religious.

The Miraculous Medal is oval. On the front, Our Lady is depicted with her arms extended. The rays of light symbolize the graces with which she showers the faithful. At the same time, she crushes the head of the infernal serpent with her virginal feet. Framing the Virgin around the edge is the prayer: "O Mary conceived without sin, pray for us who have recourse to thee."

On the reverse side, the letter "M" is surmounted with a cross. Below are the Sacred Hearts of Jesus and Mary. Encircling the whole are twelve stars that remind us of the famous words of the Apocalypse: "A woman clothed with the sun, and the moon under her feet, and on her head a crown of twelve stars."[1]

The symbols used on the Miraculous Medal summarize in an admirable way the great truths that the Catholic Church teaches about Our Lady. As an expert on the subject, Father Ricardo Rábanos C.M., wrote: "We can say that the Miraculous Medal is the most complete graphic synthesis of Mariology. As if in a panoramic view, we can contemplate in it all of Mary's titles and grandeur: the Mediation, the Co-Redemption, the divine and spiritual Maternity, the distribution of graces, the Royalty and, moreover, the Immaculate Conception."[2]

---

1. Apoc. 12:1.
2. Ricardo Rábanos, *La Inmaculada de la Medalla Milagrosa*, 409.

To understand the origins and meaning of the Miraculous Medal well, it is worthwhile knowing something of the life of Saint Catherine Labouré and the historical and political context in which she lived. Why is this context important? Because the revelations that gave origin to the Miraculous Medal, although their content is essentially religious, are profoundly related to the political events in France throughout the nineteenth century. As such, they have a certain analogy with the revelations of Our Lady in Fatima in 1917, also essentially religious. But the Fatima revelations also have important political and social implications: the prediction of the Second World War, the fall of Russia to communism and the subsequent spreading of its errors throughout the world, the future conversion of Russia, etc.

One can say that the apparitions of the Miraculous Medal in 1830 opened a cycle of great Marian manifestations that continued with La Salette in 1846, Lourdes in 1858 and culminated with Fatima in 1917.

Childhood and education of Saint Catherine Labouré to whom Our Lady revealed the Miraculous Medal

Saint Catherine Labouré was born in 1806 in Fain-lès-Moutiers in the French province of Burgundy. Her father, Pierre Labouré, owned a rural property that he worked himself. Her mother, Magdalène Gontard, belonged to a distinguished and cultured family related to the nobility of the region.

Catherine was only nine years old when her mother died. Desolate, the girl climbed onto a piece of furniture and embraced a statue of Our Lady. Weeping, she asked the Virgin to replace her mother whom she had just lost: "From now on, you will be my Mother!" In fact, from that moment on, the Most Holy Virgin's predilection for the orphan was well known.

Catherine's oldest sister, Marie-Louise, entered the Daughters of Charity of St. Vincent de Paul in 1817. From then on Catherine was responsible for the housework. To help her she had a sister two years her junior called Marie-Antoinette. Although very young, Catherine fulfilled her household duties in a most exemplary manner.

As she grew older, requests for her hand in marriage abounded, but she always refused. She had decided never to marry, because she wanted to become a spouse of Our Lord Jesus Christ.

Her religious vocation seems to have its origins in her early childhood and reaffirmed itself on the occasion of a mysterious dream she had when about eighteen years old. She dreamt that she was in the little church of Fain-lès-Moutiers and that an elderly priest, with an impressive gaze, was celebrating Mass. At the end of the Mass, the priest motioned her to approach. Afraid, she hesitated, but was fascinated by the extraordinary brilliance of his gaze. Shortly afterwards, in the same dream, she once again came across the old priest who said: "My daughter, you flee from me now, but one day you will seek me. God has designs for you, never forget this."

At the time, Catherine did not understand the dream. Only some time later when she saw a picture of Saint Vincent de Paul at the house of the Daughters of Charity in Châtillon-sur-Seine, where she went to study, did she recognize the mysterious personage of the dream. She then understood that the founder of the Daughters of Charity was calling her to be his spiritual daughter.

Saint Catherine's earthly father raised all sorts of obstacles to her entering the religious life. He not only denied his permission, but provided occasions to try to make her lose her vocation. For a whole year, she was made to help her brother who owned a restaurant for workmen in Paris. One can well imagine the dangers of such an

Catherine feeding the pigeons

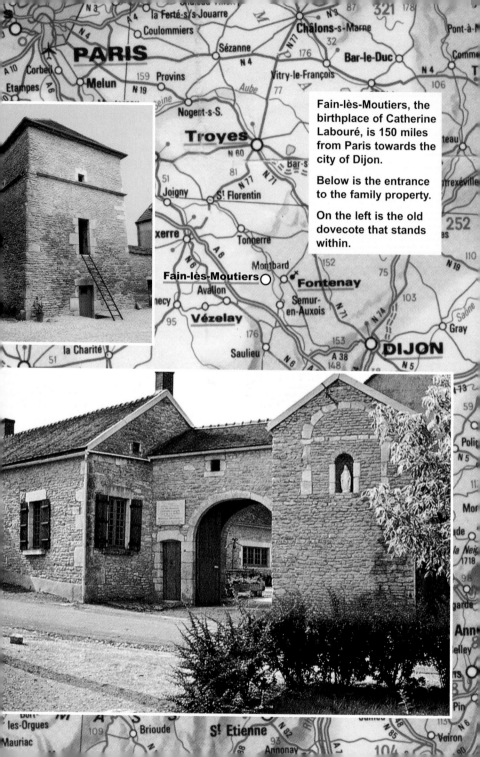

Fain-lès-Moutiers, the birthplace of Catherine Labouré, is 150 miles from Paris towards the city of Dijon.

Below is the entrance to the family property.

On the left is the old dovecote that stands within.

Left: Saint Catherine was born in this room. Next to her mother's bed is the wooden cradle that held the infant saint.

Below: The house's main room with the kitchen and its large, sturdy wood table and two chimneys.

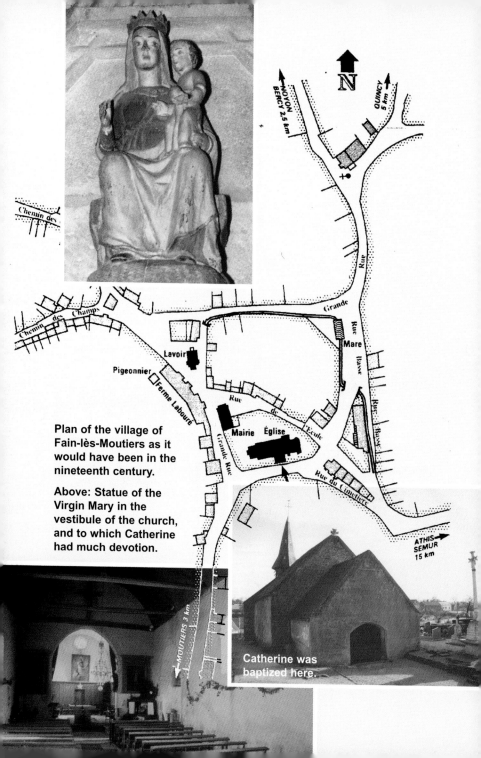

Plan of the village of Fain-lès-Moutiers as it would have been in the nineteenth century.

Above: Statue of the Virgin Mary in the vestibule of the church, and to which Catherine had much devotion.

Catherine was baptized here.

NOYON BERCY 2.5 km

QUINCY 5 km

N

Grande Rue

Rue Basse

Rue Basse

Mare

Lavoir

Pigeonnier

Ferme Labouré

Rue de l'École

Mairie

Église

Grande Rue

Rue du Cimetière

ATHIS SEMUR 15 km

Chemin des

Chemin des Champs

MOUTIERS 3 km

Right: In this chapel Catherine made her First Holy Communion.

Below right: A view of the interior of the chapel.

Below left: A picturesque scene at the entrance of the retirement home.

Catherine took special pleasure in seeing the retirement home of the Daughters of Charity in Moutiers from the road that ran in front of her family home, some two miles distant. She often rose at 4:00 o'clock in the morning to attend daily Mass there.

environment for a chaste young lady. Being blissfully ignorant of the men's jokes and gallantries, she served their tables perfectly while neither speaking nor looking at them. In the end she imposed respect.

After a long struggle, and only when she was 23 years old, did she finally obtain permission to enter the Daughters of St. Vincent de Paul in Châtillon-sur-Seine, where she was received as a postulant. Three months later in April of 1830, by now a novice, she was transferred to another house of the Congregation on the Rue du Bac in Paris, soon to become world famous.

Shortly after Catherine's arrival at Rue du Bac, the relics of Saint Vincent de Paul which had to be hidden during the dark days of the Revolution, were returned to his religious family. Enshrined in a magnificent silver reliquary, his body was transferred to the priory chapel of Saint-Lazare and into the care of his sons, the Priests of the Mission. His heart, still incorrupt 170 years after his death, was entrusted to his Daughters of Charity. The solemnity of the ceremony, the grandeur of the procession from Notre-Dame Cathedral led by the Archbishop of Paris, Monseigneur de Quélen, and accompanied by a large consort of clergy and eight bishops, and graced by the presence of His Majesty the King, all had a profound effect upon the young novice.

The following week, Catherine had the first of her supernatural visions. She narrates: "The heart of Saint Vincent appeared to me under three different forms, on three consecutive days. First it was light in color, flesh color, bespeaking peace, calm, innocence and concord. Next it was red as fire, as if to signify the charity that, by enkindling all hearts, should renew the entire community and enable it to spread to the remotest parts of the earth. Finally, I saw it as dark red, which caused me great sadness that seemed to me nearly insurmountable and, I know not why, linked to a change in the government."

With docility and confidence, Catherine told her confessor, Father Jean-Marie Aladel, about her visions. But he, fearing they were diabolical illusions or the effect of an over-excited imagination, was adamant and advised her not to take them seriously: "Do not listen to those temptations. A Sister of Charity is made to serve the poor, not to dream."

Portrait of Saint Vincent de Paul

The heart of the holy founder of the Daughters of Charity appears to Saint Catherine Labouré. Painting by Lecerf.

Solemn transferral of the relics of Saint Vincent de Paul.

Political situation of France at the time the Miraculous Medal was revealed

It is interesting to note that the young novice's sadness at seeing the darkened heart of Saint Vincent de Paul was related to a political event of the time: the change of government. A quick word about this seems appropriate. Political events can have, and frequently do have, much bearing upon the religious life of peoples. It is true that events happening in the political sphere belong to the temporal order and not to the spiritual one. However, although they are two perfectly distinct spheres, they are intimately related. This is because the good or bad ordering of temporal society generally influences the good or bad ordering of the spiritual sphere.

Body and soul are perfectly distinct in man. However, since man forms one whole, if the body is sick his soul also suffers. Because of this principle, the Catholic Church is not indifferent to political regimes. Now, the successive political transformations in France in the nineteenth century were determined ultimately by a profoundly anti-Catholic revolutionary philosophy having its origins in Humanism and the Renaissance with subsequent violent manifestations during the French Revolution.[3]

After the fall of the French monarchy in 1793 with the public beheading of King Louis XVI and his wife Queen Marie Antoinette, the tumultuous Reign of Terror began. From 1794, the Revolution suffered successive strategic retreats that ended, in 1804, with the creation of an empire by Napoleon Bonaparte that put all of Europe, from Lisbon to Moscow, into disarray.

---

3. This process had subsequent manifestations that continue until today. For those of our readers interested in knowing more about this tenacious process destroying the City of God and building the City of Man, we recommend the book *Revolution and Counter-Revolution* by Prof. Plinio Corrêa de Oliveira available from the American TFP. Call (888) 317-5571 to order.

The creation of a Napoleonic empire seemed to be a setback for the revolutionary forces. But in reality it served their cause well, because wherever the French armies went, they took with them the revolutionary spirit and the institutions originating from the Revolution of 1789. In 1806, the very year in which Saint Catherine Labouré was born, Napoleon Bonaparte declared the Holy Roman Empire, founded by Charlemagne in 800, to be extinct. More than any other, this temporal institution symbolized the order that the revolutionary forces so much wanted to destroy.

After the final defeat of Napoleon Bonaparte in 1815 came the Bourbon Restoration in France in the person of Louis XVIII. For the most part, however, the monarchies of the nineteenth century were not the same as those before 1789. Having been influenced by the liberalism and the principles of the French Revolution, they were totally different from the good and traditional organic monarchies that existed prior to the emergence of the absolutism of kings.

King Louis XVIII died in 1824 and was succeeded by his brother Charles X. By the end of July 1830, the French monarchy, shaken by the same revolutionary fermentation, suffered a further blow. As a result of a liberal revolution, Charles X was deposed and replaced by an illegitimate monarch, Louis Philippe. This was the so-called July Monarchy.

In February of 1848, a further revolution deposed Louis Philippe and installed the Second French Republic. This lasted only a short time because in 1851 the president-elect Louis-Napoleon Bonaparte (nephew of the first Napoleon) led a coup d'état, installed a new empire and proclaimed himself Emperor Napoleon III.

The Second Empire lasted only eighteen years, coincidentally the same as the July Monarchy. In 1870, Napoleon III, having been defeated by Prussia, lost his throne and the Third Republic was proclaimed. The anticlerical nature of the new regime soon manifested itself. "Clericalism is the enemy," declared Léon Gambetta, one of the most active republican leaders.

In March of 1871, when France was once again at war with Prussia, a new revolution, communist in nature, broke out in Paris. Faced with this even more radical revolutionary onslaught, the republican government seemed conservative and even counter-revolutionary. For seventy days the capital was dominated by the Commune and given over to unrestrained violence. In the midst of the chaos, Archbishop Darboy of Paris was shot dead, numerous religious were assassinated, and unspeakable sacrileges were committed in churches and convents. Finally, after a long and bloody repression, the government retook the capital and the Third Republic was consolidated.

This summary account of these events is essential to understand the context and the scope of the apparitions to Catherine Labouré.

Vision of the Most Blessed Sacrament and the first apparition of Our Lady

Let us now return to our young novice who had just received the discouraging recommendation from her confessor not to pay attention to visions. Father Aladel kept to this policy for a long time and it was a great trial for the holy religious.

During her entire novitiate, as Saint Catherine was to relate, she was privileged to see Our Lord in the Blessed Sacrament "except when I doubted." In other words, when she, in order to be faithful to her confessor, tried to resist the supposed illusion.

During one of these visions, "Our Lord appeared to me in the Blessed Sacrament as a king with a cross on His breast. At the moment of the Gospel, it seemed to me that the cross slipped down to His feet. It seemed that Our Lord was bereft of all His vestments as they fell to the ground. Then I had the darkest and saddest thoughts: the earthly king would be dethroned and despoiled of the symbols of his royalty."

This vision took place on Trinity Sunday, June 6, 1830, seven weeks before the political agitation that culminated in the dethroning of King Charles X. Illuminated by this supernatural vision, young Catherine understood that the monarch would soon lose his crown and that this would be a victory of the forces of evil in France. She deemed it necessary to warn her confessor, Father Aladel, who once again took the warning lightly.

The coronation
of Charles X in the
Cathedral of Rheims.

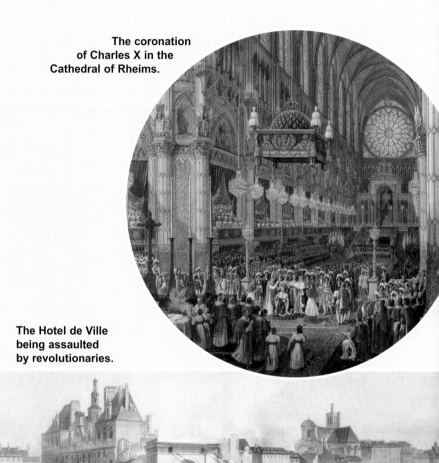

The Hotel de Ville
being assaulted
by revolutionaries.

At this time, Charles X's throne seemed more secure than ever. The future was promising for the French monarchy as it contemplated the conquest of the city of Algiers in North Africa. On the other hand, from a religious point of view, the fervor shown by the people during the transferral of the body of Saint Vincent de Paul also seemed to assure there was no psychological climate for a new revolution.

On the night of July 18, 1830, on the vigil of the feast of Saint Vincent de Paul, Saint Catherine saw Our Lady for the first time. It was her Guardian Angel, under the guise of a little boy, who took her to the Virgin. Let us once again read her own account which is impressive for its simplicity and faith:

"The novices had received a piece of Saint Vincent's linen surplice. I cut mine in half and swallowed one piece, then went to sleep with the thought that he would obtain for me the grace to see the Most Holy Virgin.

"At eleven thirty I awoke to the sound of my name being called: 'Sister Labouré! Sister Labouré!' I drew aside the curtain and saw a little boy of about four or five years of age, dressed in white and surrounded by a radiant halo, who said: 'Come to the chapel. Our Lady is there waiting for you.'

"I dressed in haste and went to the side of the little boy, who had remained standing at the head of my bed. He accompanied me keeping to my left side. All the places we went through were illuminated, which greatly surprised me. However, I was even more surprised at the door of the chapel, for it opened at once when the boy just barely touched it with the tip of his finger. And my surprise was even more complete when I saw that all the candles were alight, reminding me of Midnight Mass.

The arrow indicates the place in
the Chapel at Rue du Bac where
the apparitions took place.

Photo taken of the same Chapel of the Apparitions, 2016.

The chair in which Our Lady sat while she spoke to Saint Catherine Labouré.

Drawing depicting the sequence of the apparitions of Our Lady of Graces to Saint Catherine.

"However, I did not see the Most Holy Virgin. The little boy led me to the sanctuary next to the Spiritual Director's armchair. I knelt there, while the boy remained standing the whole time…. Finally, the moment came. The boy advised me, 'The Holy Virgin is coming; here she is.'

"I then heard something like the rustling of a silk dress, coming from beside the pulpit near the picture of Saint Joseph and ceasing over the steps of the altar on the Gospel side, on a chair like that of Saint Anne…

"At that moment, seeing the Most Holy Virgin, I rushed forward, knelt before her, and placed my hands on her knees. It was the sweetest moment of my life, but I cannot express all that I felt. Our Lady told me how I should conduct myself towards my spiritual director, and the various things that I should not say. She also told me how I should bear my sufferings by throwing myself at the foot of the altar (indicating to me the foot of the altar with her left hand as she spoke) and to open my heart there. There I would receive all the consolations I needed. Then I asked her what all the things I had seen meant, and she explained everything to me."

The conversation with Our Lady lasted for approximately one hour and a half. In another manuscript, Saint Catherine Labouré was more explicit and revealed, at least in part, what she heard from the Most Holy Virgin. First, Our Lady spoke to the young novice about a mission God wanted to confide to her, the difficulties in fulfilling it, and how she should behave towards her confessor:

"My daughter, the good God wants to give you a mission. You will suffer much, but you will overcome those sufferings by considering that you will do so for the glory of God… You will be contradicted, but you will receive grace. Do not fear. Tell everything [to your confessor] with confidence and simplicity. Have confidence, do not fear."

A little later, Our Lady began to speak of future events that soon took place:

"The times are very evil. Great calamities will befall France. The throne will be overthrown. The whole world will be disturbed with evils of all sorts (the Most Holy Virgin was very sad when saying this). But come to the foot of this altar. Here graces will be poured out over all persons, great or small, who request them with confidence and devotion."

Next Our Lady spoke about the community of the Daughters of Charity to which Saint Catherine belonged, and about the Lazarist priests, also founded by Saint Vincent de Paul:

"My daughter, I am pleased to shower this community with graces, for I love it very much. But I am saddened to see the great abuses that exist regarding regularity. The Rule is not kept. There has been too much relaxation in both communities. Relate this to the person in charge of you, even though he is not yet your superior. Later, when he is given charge of the community, he should do everything in his power to restore the Rule again. Tell him that I say he must guard against bad reading material, against the wasting of time, and against useless visits."

She then spoke anew of the terrible events that would happen in the more distant future. Forty years before their time, she predicted the agitation of the Paris Commune and the assassination of the Archbishop of Paris. And she promised her special protection for the sons and daughters of Saint Vincent de Paul during those tragic times:

"You will know my presence and the protection of God and Saint Vincent over the two communities. Have confidence! Do not lose courage. I will be with you. But this will not happen with other congregations, among whom there will be many victims. (When saying this the Most Holy Virgin had tears in her eyes.) There will be victims among the clergy of Paris: the Archbishop himself will die. (At these words, she again wept.)

"My daughter, the cross will be despised and thrown down. Blood will flow. The side of Our Lord will be reopened. The streets will flow with blood. The Archbishop will be deprived of his vestments. (For a time, the Most Holy Virgin could speak no more and her face was overcome by sorrow.) My daughter, the whole world will suffer."

Saint Catherine continues: "At these words I wondered when this would happen, and I understood very well: in forty years."

As always, Catherine faithfully told everything to her confessor. Once again he was severe, saying that this was "pure fantasy" and reprimanded the novice: "If you want to honor Our Lady, imitate Her virtues and guard yourself against your imagination." But the incredulous confessor could not help but be struck with terror, because one week later the prophecies began to be fulfilled.

By July 26, news arrived of mayhem in the streets and within a few days King Charles X had been deposed. Besides being liberal, the revolution of 1830 was also violently anti-clerical. Several churches were profaned, monasteries and convents were invaded, and priests and nuns persecuted. But the Lazarists and the Daughters of St. Vincent de Paul went through this critical period unharmed just as Our Lady had promised.

During the second apparition, Our Lady reveals the Miraculous Medal

Four months later, on November 27, 1830, Our Lady appeared again to Saint Catherine. She taught her the devotion to the medal that, because of its prodigies, Catholics would call the Miraculous Medal. Let us once again listen to the words of the saint:

"I saw the Most Holy Virgin; she was at the level of the picture of Saint Joseph. She was of medium height, standing and dressed in a silk robe, as white as the glow of the dawn... She wore a white veil on her head that extended to her feet and covered her entirely. Through this veil, I saw her hair parted in the middle and held by a piece of lace of about an inch in width. Her face was uncovered, totally uncovered. She stood on a half sphere... and had in her hands a golden globe that represented the world. Her hands were raised to the height of her waist in a very natural way and her eyes looked up to Heaven... Her face was extremely beautiful. I would not know how to describe it... And then, suddenly, I saw rings appear on her fingers, covered with stones, some more beautiful than others, some larger and some smaller, and shedding rays, each more beautiful than the other. The most beautiful rays came from the largest stones, always extending down-

A painting depicting the apparition that occurred on November 27, 1830.

30 THE MIRACULOUS MEDAL

wards, filling the lower area. I could no longer see her feet…. At this moment, as I was contemplating her, the Most Holy Virgin lowered her eyes and looked at me. A voice spoke within me:

"'The globe you see represents the whole world, particularly France… and everyone in it…'

"Here I do not know how to express what I felt and saw, the beauty, the brilliance, the splendid rays…

"'The rays of light from my hands are the graces I shower on those who request them.' I understood how pleasing it is to pray to the Most Holy Virgin and how generous she is to those who pray to her, how many graces she grants to those who pray for them, the joy she feels granting them…

"A sort of oval frame formed around the Most Holy Virgin, with the following words on the upper part: 'O Mary conceived without sin, pray for us who have recourse to thee' written in gold letters. The inscription, in a semicircle, began at the right hand passing over the head and ended at the left hand…

"Then a voice said: 'Have a medal struck upon this model. Everyone who wears it, when it is blessed, will receive great graces especially if they wear it around their neck. Graces will be abundant for those who wear it with confidence…'"

The following month, Saint Catherine saw Our Lady once again. She appeared as She had in November holding the golden globe with a small cross on top, also of gold, and the same light came from the rings but with different intensities.

"It is impossible to express what I understood at the moment when the Most Holy Virgin offered the globe to God," the seer wrote. And then added, "As I was enraptured in the contemplation of the Most Holy Virgin, a voice resounded at the bottom of my heart: 'These rays symbolize the graces the Most Holy Virgin obtains for those people who ask for them.'"

Saint Catherine noticed that no rays were coming from some of the stones on the rings. A voice enlightened her: "The stones from which nothing comes are graces men forget to ask me."

The first medals are struck and stupendous prodigies take place

Saint Catherine's confessor, however, continued to be incredulous. He considered her to be a visionary not to be taken seriously. For more than a year, Saint Catherine indefatigably insisted with the priest that medals be struck as Our Lady had requested. But he inflexibly continued to resist.

One day Father Aladel was asked to accompany his superior to an audience with the Archbishop of Paris, Monseigneur de Quélen. Taking advantage of the opportunity, he informed the prelate what was happening at Rue du Bac without revealing the name of the visionary. This audience took place in January of 1832, ending a long period of affliction for the holy religious.

Contrary to Father Aladel's expectations, the Archbishop immediately endorsed the casting of the medal. Encouraged in turn, Father Aladel changed his attitude and four months later, in May, placed an order for 20,000 medals with Vachette House.

As the first medals were being made, a terrible epidemic of cholera, coming from Eastern Europe, struck Paris.

The disease first appeared on March 26, 1832 and continued until the middle of the year. By April 1, 79 people had died; by the next day, the number had risen to 168, by the third day of April, 216. By April 9, the death toll had risen to 861. In total, the official records report that 18,400 people perished. In reality, the number was much greater because the official statistics and the media purposely under-estimated the numbers to avoid even greater panic.

On June 30, Vachette House delivered the first 1,500 medals cast and the Daughters of Charity began distributing them among those afflicted. The epidemic receded immediately and the numerous prodigies that followed quickly made the Miraculous Medal world famous.

The Archbishop, who had received some of the first medals, immediately obtained an extraordinary grace through them and became an enthusiastic promoter and protector of the new devotion.

Above left: Father Aladel, Saint Catherine's confessor, ordered the first 20,000 medals.

Above right: One of the first medals struck.

Right: Monseigneur de Quélen, Archbishop of Paris, was an enthusiastic propagator of the new devotion.

Below: A sketch from the epoch shows the Archbishop distributing medals to those stricken by the cholera epidemic in 1832.

Pope Gregory XVI also received a package of medals and began distributing them to people who visited him.

By 1836, more than 15 million medals had been struck and distributed throughout the world. In 1842, this figure reached 100 million. From the furthest corners of the earth arrived reports of extraordinary graces obtained through the medal: cures, conversions, protection against imminent dangers and many other events.

But in January of 1842, a spectacular conversion highlighted the Miraculous Medal in a special way.

The conversion of Alphonse Ratisbonne

Alphonse Ratisbonne was a young Jew from a family of well-established bankers in Strasbourg. He also was socially prominent due to his wealth and blood ties to the Rothchilds.

In 1827, Alphonse's older brother, Théodore, converted to Catholicism and entered the priesthood, thus breaking with his family whose hopes now lay in the young Alphonse born in 1814.

Alphonse was intelligent and well mannered, had completed his law degree and was engaged to a young Jewish lady, his niece. He was 27 years old and, before marrying, he wanted to take an extended trip to Italy and the East. Upon his return, he planned to marry and assume his responsibilities in his family's banking business.

God, however, had other plans for him in Rome.

Alphonse was not a practising Jew. He nourished a profound hatred for the Catholic Church, especially because of the resentment his whole family had due to their firstborn's defection. Alphonse said he would never change religion. But if one day he were to change, he would become a Protestant, never a Catholic.

While in Rome, Ratisbonne visited works of art, as well as some Catholic churches out of cultural curiosity. These visits hardened his anti-Catholic stance.

He also visited an old schoolmate and close friend named Gustave de Bussières. Gustave was a Protestant and on many occasions had tried, in vain, to win Alphonse over to his religious convictions. In Gustave's house, Alphonse was introduced to his friend's brother, Baron Théodore de Bussières, who had just recently converted to Catholicism. Baron Théodore, in turn, was a close friend of Father Théodore Ratisbonne. Because of these two circumstances, Alphonse greatly disliked him.

Thus it was only upon the eve of his departure from Rome that Alphonse reluctantly decided to fulfill the social obligation of the time of leaving his calling card at the Baron's house as a farewell gesture. Having resolved to avoid a meeting with this new acquaintance, he intended to leave his card discreetly and depart straight away. The Baron's Italian servant, however, did not understand his French and ushered him into the parlor while he went to call the Baron. The latter greeted the young Jew and immediately established cordial relations, while trying to attract him to the Catholic Faith.

With much insistence, he was able to persuade Alphonse to delay his departure from Rome in order to attend a ceremony to be held at St. Peter's Basilica. He further succeeded in persuading Ratisbonne to accept a Miraculous Medal and to promise to copy down a very beautiful prayer: the *Memorare*. Had this action not been inspired by grace, it would have been utterly indiscreet.

Alphonse could hardly contain his anger at the Baron's boldness in proposing these things to him, but decided to take everything good-heartedly, hoping, as he later declared, to write a book about his travels. In this book, the Baron would appear as nothing more than an eccentric man.

On January 18, a close friend of the Baron de Bussières died. He was Count de La Ferronays, the former French ambassador to the Holy See and a man of great virtue and piety. On the eve of his sudden death, La Ferronays was talking to Bussières about Ratisbonne and, at the request of Bussières, prayed the *Memorare* one hundred times for his conversion. It is even possible that he offered his life to God for the conversion of the young banker.

Around midday on January 20, the Baron de Bussières went to the Church of Sant'Andrea delle Fratte to arrange for his deceased friend's funeral to be held the following day. Ratisbonne reluctantly went along,

Apparition of Our Lady to Alphonse Ratisbonne, Basilica of Sant'Andrea delle Fratte, Rome.

Marble bust of Alphonse Ratisbonne next to the altar where he saw Our Lady.

Above: The altar where Our Lady of the Miracle appeared to the young Jewish lawyer in the Basilica of Sant'Andrea delle Fratte.

Left: Map showing the location of the church in the city of Rome.

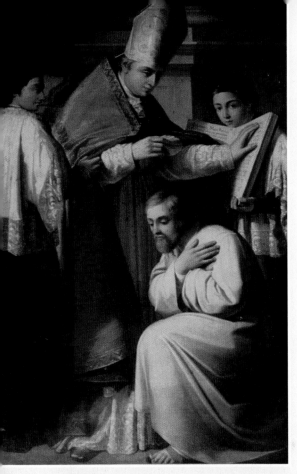

The baptism of Alphonse Ratisbonne, Basilica Sant'Andrea delle Fratte.

Théodore Ratisbonne

Count de La Ferronays

Théodore de Bussiéres

making violent criticisms of the Church and mocking Catholic practices. When they arrived at the church, the Baron left him alone for a few minutes and entered the sacristy to see about the funeral arrangements. Alphonse decided to look around and went up one of the side aisles since he could not cross over due to the preparations for the Count's funeral in the central nave.

When the Baron returned just a few minutes later, he did not find Alphonse where he had left him. After much searching, he found him on the other side of the church kneeling close to an altar, weeping. He no longer found a Jew, but a convert who ardently desired baptism.

Ratisbonne himself tells us what happened in those few minutes: "I had only been in the church a short while when, all of a sudden, I felt totally uneasy for no apparent reason. I raised my eyes and saw that the whole building had disappeared. Only one side chapel had, so to say, gathered all the light. In the midst of this splendor, the Virgin Mary appeared standing on the altar. She was grandiose, brilliant, full of majesty and sweetness, just as she is in the Miraculous Medal. An irresistible force attracted me to her. The Virgin made a gesture with her hand indicating I was to kneel and as if saying 'very good!' Although, she did not say anything, I understood everything."

Ratisbonne never could explain how, being left in one of the side aisles before the apparition, he was afterwards found in the other, since the central nave was obstructed. However, in face of the magnitude of the miracle of his conversion, this was a mere detail.

The news of such an unexpected conversion, so fulminating and complete, immediately spread and caused a great commotion throughout Europe.

Pope Gregory XVI wished to meet the young convert and received him paternally. He ordered a detailed investigation with all the rigor required by canon law. The conclusion was that it was truly an authentic miracle.

Having taken the name Maria Alphonse at baptism, Ratisbonne wished to become a Jesuit and was ordained in 1847. After a while and at the suggestion of Pope Pius IX, he left the Jesuits and joined his brother Théodore in founding the Congregation of Our Lady of Sion, an order dedicated to the conversion of the Jews.

Father Théodore spread his congregation throughout France and England, while Father Maria Alphonse went to the Holy Land. In Jerusalem he established a house of the congregation where the praetorium of Pilate had formerly stood. The two brothers died in 1884, both with the fame of exceptional virtues.

Saint Catherine Labouré's great secret

The wide distribution of the Miraculous Medal powerfully contributed to the creation of a climate of generalized fervor towards Mary's Immaculate Conception. It was this climate that encouraged the Supreme Magisterium of the Church to proclaim the Immaculate Conception as a dogma in 1854 at St. Peter's Basilica in a splendid ceremony that overjoyed Catholics throughout the world.

However, Saint Catherine, who in 1831 had been transferred from Rue du Bac to the Retirement Home of Enghien, in the Parisian neighborhood of Reuilly, did not put on any airs in her behavior and duties. She cared for the poor as an ordinary nun without telling anyone, or insinuating that she was the messenger whom Mary Most Holy had chosen to reveal the Miraculous Medal to the world.

Among her duties, she cared for the needs of the elderly and the infirm, as well as tending to the dairy and the cleaning and care of the clothes and linens. At one time, she was also responsible for the kitchen.

Above: A sketch of the front of the Retirement Home of Enghien in Reuilly, Paris where Saint Catherine spent the greater part of her life performing the duties of a Daughter of Charity. Below left: Photograph taken in the Home's garden. Below right: 77 Rue de Reuilly and its location in Paris (map).

Everyone knew that a former novice at Rue du Bac had received the revelations, but, for many years only Father Aladel knew the identity of the seer. Not even the Mother Superior of the convent knew, and neither did the Archbishop of Paris, who as we saw was a supporter of the new devotion from the beginning. She was even unknown to the Holy Father, Pope Gregory XVI, likewise a protector and promoter of the Miraculous Medal. Father Aladel did not reveal it to anyone, alleging he was under the seal of confession. Even Father Alphonse Ratisbonne was frustrated in his attempts to meet the religious who, like himself, had received the extraordinary grace of seeing the Mother of God.

Saint Catherine herself never mentioned anything to her religious companions. When the first medals were ready and distributed to the sisters, the saint received hers just like everyone else.

During the tragic days of the Paris Commune, however, her attitude was very different from her co-religious. Danger surrounded the convent and the nuns understandably lived in constant fear. Only Sister Catherine, reassured by her visions forty years earlier that nothing would happen to the nuns, was calm and confident. "The Virgin will watch over us; nothing bad will happen to us," she assured her companions.

The revolutionaries even invaded the Retirement Home of Enghien and expelled the nuns. Saint Catherine, who was at this time head of the house in the absence of the Mother Superior, remained imperturbable and declared that they would all be back in one month, by May 31, and that the house would be intact, having been watched over by the Virgin herself. Subsequent events proved her right.

Only at the end of her life, years after the death of Father Aladel, did Saint Catharine Labouré feel supernaturally impelled to speak to her Mother Superior, Sister Jeanne Duffès, about a request of Our Lady that had not yet been fulfilled and which we will mention later. This was the only time she had revealed to anyone, other than her confessor, her role as the messenger of Mary Most Holy.

By this time, because of an understandable curiosity among the younger nuns, many were certain that Sister Catherine had been the privileged seer. They reached this conclusion notwithstanding the

Painting by J.M. Durand, donated to the Daughters of Charity by the heirs of Phillippe Meugniot.

Catherine fearlessly distributed medals to the soldiers of the Commune who had invaded the retirement home.

Below: The desk and chair in the reception hall normally staffed by Saint Catherine. Behind is the clock that was there during her lifetime.

Above: Photograph of the reception hall at Reuilly.

fact that Saint Catherine had never said anything to betray the great
secret of her life, and this was remarked upon discreetly throughout
the community.

*   *   *

On the Miraculous Medal as we know it, Our Lady appears with
her arms outstretched and with her hands open. From her fingers
come the graces for the faithful. In Saint Catherine's manuscripts,
however, it is clear that Our Lady's desire in 1830 was to be represented with a globe in her hands with the attitude of one who is offering it to God. And it was from the rings on her fingers that the graces
to mankind poured forth.

Why was the medal changed?

During the beatification process of Sister Catherine Labouré, the
subject was discussed. Everything seems to indicate that it was due to
a lamentable simplification decided upon by her confessor. Possibly
Father Aladel was afraid such an unusual representation of the Virgin
would be thought odd in Rome. In any case, it is undeniable that, even
in the medal's present form, Mary Most Holy has granted abundant
graces. Therefore, no change should be made to its well-known form.

When, in 1832, the first medals were distributed to the nuns at
Rue du Bac, Saint Catherine Labouré, without insinuating she was the
seer, commented: "Now this medal must be distributed."

Just before her death in 1876, Saint Catherine let her opinion be
known to her Mother Superior, Sister Jeanne Duffés, who was per-
plexed by the globe not being on the medal. Saint Catherine said: "Oh!
The medal should not be changed!"

By this time, more than one billion Miraculous Medals had been
made and were spreading graces around the whole world.

Saint Catherine Labouré's great martyrdom

To conclude the life of Saint Catherine Labouré—hidden to the
eyes of men, but great in the eyes of God—we must say something

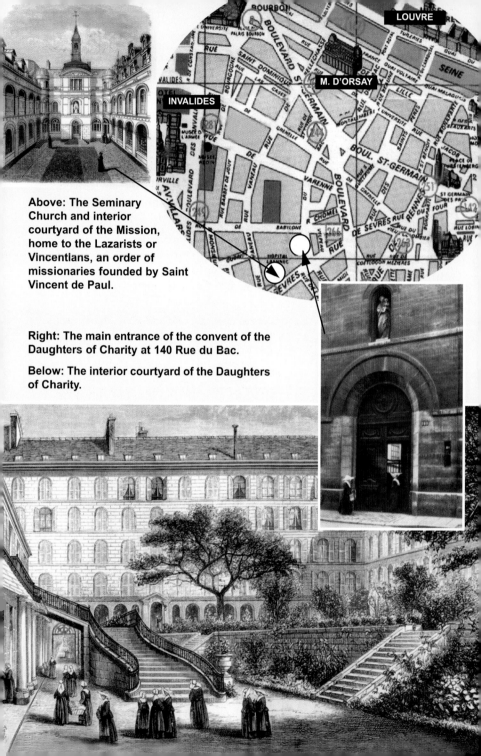

LOUVRE

M. D'ORSAY

INVALIDES

Above: The Seminary Church and interior courtyard of the Mission, home to the Lazarists or Vincentlans, an order of missionaries founded by Saint Vincent de Paul.

Right: The main entrance of the convent of the Daughters of Charity at 140 Rue du Bac.

Below: The interior courtyard of the Daughters of Charity.

regarding what she herself declared as being the martyrdom of her life.

As we have seen, Our Lady was not depicted on the Miraculous Medal with a globe in her hands and with the rays coming from the rings just as she had seen in 1830. However, Saint Catherine had always insisted with Father Aladel, as well as with her successive confessors, that a statue be made just as Our Lady had appeared and placed on the spot where Our Lady had appeared to her.

"I have been tormented now for two years and compelled to tell you that, as I have asked, an altar should be erected on the same spot where the Most Holy Virgin appeared to me. It will be privileged with many graces and indulgences and there will be an abundance of graces for you and the whole community, as well as for all those who come to pray to her," she wrote to Father Aladel in August, 1841.

For decades the saint was unable to convince Father Aladel and her subsequent confessors to have this statue made. This made her suffer very much.

Only in 1876, the year of her death, was she finally able to convince her Mother Superior to have a statue of the Virgin with the globe in her hands made; but it did not have the rays coming from the rings as she wished. When they presented the statue to her, Catherine could not hide her disappointment: "Our Lady was much more beautiful than this," she said.

On the last day of the same year, she surrendered her most pure soul to God Whom she would contemplate face to face for all eternity. He was the Lord Whom she had lovingly served her whole life, as well as His Holy and Immaculate Mother, whose devotion she had contributed so much to spread.

Her body was buried on January 3, 1877 and exhumed in 1933 when it was found to be incorrupt, still whole and flexible. The doctor in charge of the exhumation, seeing the body so flexible, had the idea of opening Saint Catherine's eyelids. Upon doing so, he was startled to see a marvel: not only did her eyelids open easily, but also her blue eyes that had contemplated Mary Most Holy were still clear and beautiful.

Saint Catherine Labouré's body now lies in a reliquary under the

The first statue of the Virgin of the Globe in the retirement home of Reuilly near Saint Catherine's room.

altar erected on the spot where Our Lady appeared. There she can be seen and venerated by the faithful who flock to Rue du Bac from around the world.

In 1894, our Holy Mother Church established the liturgical feast of Our Lady of the Miraculous Medal with its own Mass and Office on November 27.

The process of beatification of Catherine Labouré was introduced in 1907 and came to a close on May 28, 1933 when Pius XI, in St. Peter's Basilica, solemnly declared her Blessed. Fourteen years later, on July 27, 1947, Pius XII canonized her.

In 1980, the year of the 150th anniversary of the revelation of the Miraculous Medal, Pope Saint John Paul II went as a pilgrim to the place of the apparitions.

The golden globe: Symbol of the royalty of Mary, symbol of the Reign of Mary

It is now opportune to reflect on the meaning of the golden globe in Our Lady's hands, which Saint Catherine Labouré had so much insisted upon.

Evidently, the fact that Our Lady carries the globe in her hands signifies her dominion over the entire world, over blessed France, the firstborn daughter of the Church, in particular, and over souls individually as well. This is an affirmation of the effective royalty of Our Lady over the world, over nations and over souls.

Furthermore, the act by which Our Lady offers the globe to God, representing her royalty, obviously constitutes a most agreeable token of homage in His eyes. It is the most exalted of creatures that offers Him the whole universe, in other words, the whole of His creation.

Symbolically, the historical era foreseen by Saint Louis-Marie de Montfort—the great Marian apostle of modern times—could not be better depicted.

"When will that happy day come," he asked "when God's Mother is enthroned in men's hearts as Queen, subjecting them to the dominion

Painting of Saint Catherine Labouré on her deathbed.

The bed on which Saint Catherine died, December 31, 1876.

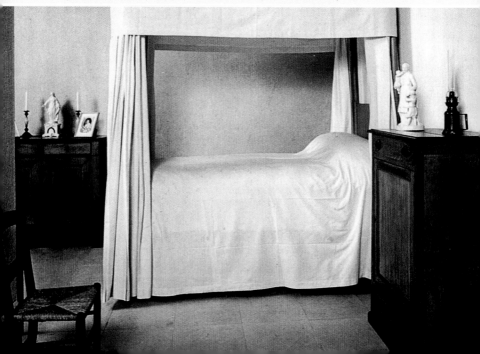

of her great and princely Son? When will souls breathe Mary as the body breathes air? When that time comes wonderful things will happen on earth. The Holy Spirit, finding his dear Spouse present again in souls, will come down into them with great power. He will fill them with his gifts, especially wisdom, by which they will produce wonders of grace. My dear friend, when will that happy time come, that age of Mary, when many souls, chosen by Mary and given to her by the most High God, will hide themselves completely in the depths of her soul, becoming living copies of her, loving and glorifying Jesus? That day will dawn only when the devotion I teach is understood and put into practice. *Ut adveniat regnum tuum, adveniat regnum Mariae.* Lord, that your kingdom come, may the reign of Mary come!"[4]

Saint Catherine Labouré seemed to have this luminous future reality in mind when she wrote these prophetically inspired words: "Oh! How beautiful it will be when we hear: Mary is Queen of the Universe, particularly of France! And the children, with transports of joy, will cry, 'and of each person in particular!' This will be an era of peace, joy, and happiness that will last a long time. The image of the Most Holy Virgin will be carried on standards around the world."

This same luminous reality was evidently what Our Lady at Fatima also had in mind when, after great chastisements and trials for humanity, she concluded her message with these words of hope: "Finally, my Immaculate Heart will triumph."

It is interesting to note how Our Lady at Fatima also appeared with a golden globe, a small one hanging from her neck. It is the same external sign of Her universal royalty that men persist in not acknowledging, but that she, in the not-too-distant future, will affirm in a sovereign and maternal manner.

---

4. de Montfort, Louis-Marie, *A Treatise on the True Devotion to the Blessed Virgin*, no. 217.

PART II

First graces obtained with the spreading of the Miraculous Medal

Having considered the historic origins of the Miraculous Medal and its meaning, let us now turn our attention to some of the amazing prodigies that occurred in Europe, in the East and in the Americas through this medal.

It would be impossible to narrate them all in the present volume for lack of space; so many are the blessings Our Lady bestows upon those devoted to her medal. However, we thought it worthwhile to reproduce some accounts of graces received around the world in the first years of distribution of the medal to give you a good idea of the abundance and variety of the graces received through the Miraculous Medal. We hope this will also help you to understand how appropriate it is for the difficult days in which we live.

These testimonies have been taken from a book written by Father Aladel, Saint Catherine Labouré's confessor. The book was edited and completed by another Lazarist priest, who preferred to remain anonymous. He did this after the author's death, as well as that of the seer.[5] We will make use of the excellent translation of Dr. Francisco d'Azeredo Teixeira d'Aguilar, Count of Samodães, edited in Porto in 1884. We have taken the liberty to do some light editing to facilitate the comprehension of the text for today's reader.[6]

We hope these testimonies will encourage you, when in similar difficulties, to likewise make use of the Miraculous Medal and to confidently invoke the protection of Our Lady of Graces.

Of course, the Miraculous Medal should not be used as a lucky charm as if it had magical qualities. The devout Catholic should use it in a spirit of faith, bearing in mind that the best way to obtain graces and favors from God is by living a life that is pleasing to Him, by fulfilling His Commandments, and through prayer and the frequent use of the Sacraments.

5. Jean-Marie Aladel, C.M., *La Médaille Miraculeuse—Origine, Histoire, Diffusion, Résultats*. Édition revue et augmentée (Paris: Pillet et Dumoulin, 1881).

6. Francisco d'Azeredo Teixeira d'Aguilar, *A Medalha Miraculosa—sua origem, história, diffusão e resultados* or *Nossa Senhora das Graças, e os Actos da sua Misericórdia*, a revised and augmented edition based on that of Fr. Jean-Marie Aladel of the Congregation of the Mission, prefaced and translated into Portuguese (Porto: Imprensa Commercial, 1884).

The cure of a sick person in Châlons-sur-Marne, France (1834)

Father Bégin, an eyewitness to this cure that took place in Saint-Maur where he was chaplain, wrote a report in which he attested to the following facts: a) that the sick person was gravely ill; b) that she was cured on March 14, 1834; and c) that she declared that she only used the medal and prayer.

One hundred witnesses from the nursing home signed this document.

Mrs. C.H., a 70-year-old widow, had been admitted in impoverished circumstances to the nursing home of Saint-Maur because of a bad fall on August 7, 1833. She walked with great difficulty and even with the help of a crutch needed someone's arm for support. She also found it hard to sit and only with great difficulty was she able to rise again. It was almost impossible for her to climb stairs, as she had to hold on to whatever she could to do so. She could not bend down or kneel, and had to drag her left leg, as that was where the problem lay. This was her unhappy state of health in the first days of March of 1834.

Nevertheless a happy piece of news gave her hope. At the beginning of January, they told her of a medal that was reported to be miraculous. They described it as having, on one side, Mary crushing the infernal serpent and showering graces from her hands symbolized by rays of light with the invocation: "O Mary conceived without sin, pray for us who have recourse to thee." On the reverse of the medal were depicted the Sacred Hearts of Jesus and Mary and the letter "M" with a cross on top.

They also told her of marvelous things that had happened. From that moment she felt her heart enkindled with the consoling hope of finding some relief that the wearing of this medal promised to her, and she could not wait for the moment she would receive one.

However, it took a long time to obtain one! Finally, on March 6, she received the much longed-for medal as a gift from Heaven. She then went to confession in order to dispose herself to receive the favor she desired. The following day, the first Friday of the month, after receiving Holy Communion, she started a novena to the Sacred

Hearts of Jesus and Mary. She venerated the medal, which she wore around her neck, twenty times a day. But the Lord tested her faith and confidence repeatedly during the nine days of the novena. Her pains increased a lot, but this only fortified her faith and confidence. As a result, in a short while, she obtained a happy answer to her requests. After only seven days of the novena, she felt free from the painful infirmities she had suffered so cruelly for seven months. We cannot describe the surprise and admiration of everyone on the morning of March 14 upon seeing this woman walk about unaided when the previous evening she had been crippled. She was able to bend down, kneel, go up and down stairs. Everyone cried out: "Miracle!" and was greatly edified by such a prodigious cure. They congratulated her on such a great grace from God and Mary Most Holy.

The Mother Superior, who had taken care of her innumerable times since she had been taken ill and daily witnessed her sufferings, wanted a *Te Deum* to be sung by the whole community in the house chapel to celebrate solemnly this extraordinary grace. The sick lady remained cured and no longer felt the effects of her former infirmity.

The bishop of Châlons also added his signature to the document:

"We certify that the testimony of Father Bégin should be taken as wholly trustworthy, as well as that of the nuns and so many others who were eye witnesses and spoke according to their consciences without any other interest except that of stating the truth.
Châlons, May 30, 1834
+ M.S.F.V., Bishop of Châlons."

The cure of Mrs. Joubert in Limoges, France (1834)

Account written by Father Poinsel, Vicar-General of Limoges.

Glory to God and Honor to Mary!
On February 10, 1834, Mrs. Joubert, 29 years old and a person of sound faith, was instantaneously cured of a painful and very grave illness.

For more than one year, she held her arm up against her chest because of an illness that could not be diagnosed and that could be felt from the shoulder blade to the hand. The infirmity was so grave that the arm seemed dead and was useless. To move it, the utmost precautions needed to be taken and, in spite of all care, the pains were so terrible that the lady could not bear them. They called the sickness gouty, inflammatory and gangrenous rheumatism. The doctors used baths, poultices, all types of liniments, unsuccessful treatments that, instead of relieving the pain, only increased her torment and varied the torture. Even amputation was discussed: "May it be God's will that only one arm needs to go," a doctor stated. He could not hide his unease and fear that she would die in the spring as the affected arm looked pale, discolored and was a horrible sight to behold.

The young lady, a devout Christian, was resigned to her fate and fortified herself in her suffering by contemplating the Holy Cross. Knowing how her sickness was advancing, she only thought of dying the precious death of the just. At this point in time she was told about the medal and how she should wear it with confidence while making a novena of prayers to Mary.

She accepted and began her novena. On the last day of the novena she went to confession, which coincided with her customary day of doing so, which was every eight days. While recollecting herself in a humble and contrite spirit and as she received absolution, she felt something physical and extraordinary happening with her incurable arm that suddenly became free and without pain.

"I did not know where I was. I had the impression that a rope, tightly wound around my arm, had been loosened, one knot at a time. Afterwards I felt well. My surprise and joy knew no bounds and I cannot even express them."

Arriving back home, she first felt like exclaiming: "Miracle, light one, two candles. Come, come see the miracle! I can move my arm, it lives and I am cured!" There was great joy among the whole family! They gathered round her, looked at her, felt her, made her move her arm in every direction, pick up objects, etc. The whole family, deeply moved and crying, knelt and recited a hymn of thanksgiving, the *Te Deum*. Since that day, one year ago now, the arm has remained healthy. The doctor was surprised by the event which would be very difficult to attribute to hidden and sudden natural causes. And, furthermore, what is nature without the intervention and action of God? Only He commands nature, makes it live and die according to His will. One does not need too many explanations. Faith leads us to acknowledge a special grace from God here through the intercession of Mary, our good and sweet Mother, our refuge and mediatrix, to whom we should surrender ourselves with confidence.

This is the simple and conscientious report of the event. It has been corroborated by the declarations of the interested person, that I, the undersigned, have received in the presence of an intelligent and capable eyewitness who cared for the arm many times and through his ability and long experience is able to assess the danger.

February 14, 1835
Poinsel, Vicar-General.

These details are further confirmed in letters written by both the mother and the daughter of the Joubert family, as well as by the Mother Superior of the Daughters of Charity of Limoges and by Mr. Dumonteil, the family lawyer and friend.

The conversion and cure of a dying person in Bologna, Italy (1836)

Testimony of a parish priest of Bologna on February 8, 1836.

There was a young man in my parish, 27 years of age, who lived a dissolute life. In order to have fewer impediments to his excesses, he had left the family home. Some time later he became gravely ill with pneumonia. Dr. Giovanni Pulioli, a distinguished doctor, treated him; but the virulence of the illness was stronger than the medicine of the day.

The youth was left in a lamentable state, unable to move. By then he was living scandalously with a woman and had declared, from the beginning of the illness, that he would not consent to a priest being called. The illness worsened and those attending him warned others of the danger.

My chaplain went to visit him and exhorted him to put an end to the scandal through marriage; but he failed to convince the young man. I went there and spoke with him about legitimizing the union, rather than breaking it up; but I found him to be in a state of complete religious indifferentism. Despite my every effort to persuade him, I also failed. I then thought it better to allow him to reflect a little while and to return another day to find out his decision. In the meantime, I asked him to have recourse to the Most Holy Virgin, refuge of sinners; and, without telling him, I placed a Miraculous Medal in his pillow and departed.

I did not need to return to the house of my own accord; the sick youth himself called me through his mother with whom he had already reconciled himself. He told me that he had reasons, which were justified, for not speaking personally with the woman with whom he had been living, and requested I ask her to leave. The unfortunate woman condescended and left.

Once I had accomplished this, I told the sick youth how happy I was. When I presented the medal to him, he began to kiss it with feelings of sincere gratitude, even though the state of his health was extremely grave. He then showed signs of sincere repentance and confessed his sins, received the Holy Viaticum and Extreme Unction, because we expected him to die at any moment. This took place on January 19, 1836.

The young man felt the greatest tranquility, which he attributed to the Most Holy Virgin. From then on he started to feel better and had totally recuperated within a few days. He still perseveres in his good resolutions and is full of love for his Heavenly benefactress whose medal he keeps as something precious, frequently kissing it with great devotion.

I myself witnessed these events and I write not only with the young man's approval, but at his request, for as this miracle took place through the intercession of Mary Most Holy, so may this account serve to give greater glory of God.

To this written testimony I have appended the medical report proving the sickness and the cure.

The prodigious cure of a child in Italy (1836)

February 22, 1836

F. Paolo de Magistris was 7 years old when in November of 1835 he became ill with a fever which the doctors diagnosed as gastric-biliousness. It was of such gravity that it was feared the boy would die. After three weeks, his nerves became affected and the sick child, now in a state of deep lethargy, lost consciousness. His afflicted parents, seeing the tenacity of the sickness, notwithstanding all the remedies applied, considered they had lost their child. On January 9th, in the afternoon, Extreme Unction was administered and the parish priest thought he had but a few hours to live.

However someone arrived and mentioned the Miraculous Medal brought from France by the Lazarist Fathers. They immediately procured one and, with much faith, placed it on the boy while those present recited the *Ave Maris Stella* on their knees. No sooner had the prayer been finished, than the boy began to improve and, in a little while, was out of danger. With this their confidence in the medal increased. So they resolved to make a novena in honor of the Most Holy Virgin, during which the illness was gradually cured.

The parents, as well as everyone else who saw this, including the doctor, attested to the deplorable state to which the boy had been reduced. Only a miracle, determined by the application of the medal, could have saved him.

The cure of a person with dropsy in Switzerland (1836)

Account given at Soleure on January 19, 1836.

Batista, who worked in a sawmill, and who you met when he was in this city, was obliged to stay in bed for two months. Dropsy was slowly killing him. One of our best doctors, who was treating him, told the family there was no further hope for Batista. They therefore consulted Dr. Gougelmann from Attyswill, which is about three miles from Soleure. Upon examining the sick man, he likewise agreed [with the prognosis]. The man's wife was prostrate with anguish. Seeing her distress, a pious woman gave her a Miraculous Medal. The legs, arms and whole body of the poor man were dreadfully swollen. He breathed with difficulty and could not move, and since he lay on his back and elbows, these developed sores. He was expected to die at any moment.

His confessor visited him and told him of the prodigies worked by the medal. The sick man then began reading aloud a pamphlet about the medal, to the great astonishment of his confessor, as well as his wife, who were witnesses to the fact that, moments earlier, he could not speak. He read the pamphlet from cover to cover.

The sick man's wife, overcome with fatigue, decided to get some rest. His children were in a room next door awaiting the sad news of their father's death. Around 3 o'clock in the morning, the sick father fell asleep. Upon awakening he felt so well that he wanted to get up out of bed and throw himself on his knees at the foot of the crucifix to give thanks to Our Lord and His Holy Mother, which indeed he did.

When his wife awoke and did not see him, she called out to ask where he was. "I am well," Batista answered. "The Most Holy Virgin has cured me." Then she saw him kneeling in the room. The children came in haste, thinking their father was uttering his last breath, but found him restored to health with all the wounds healed. Imagine this family's joy and the effect the news had on a great number of people. Since then poor Batista has been well.

The cure of a boy from 's-Hertogenbosch, Holland (1836)

In issue no. 68 of the Dutch journal Noord Brabander, *which is printed in 's-Hertogenbosch (Bois-le-Duc) in the province of North Brabant, can be found the following story of an extraordinary cure attributed to the Most Holy Virgin:*

June 6, 1836

On April 25, Francis Wenmakers, who was 14 years old, fell from a height of some fifteen feet. The impact produced a concussion and the almost total paralysis of the lungs, larynx and esophagus. As a consequence, the boy could not take any medicine as he was not even able to swallow liquids. In due course, he lost consciousness.

The doctors were closely monitoring his symptoms and paying particular attention to the clarity of his gaze, but they had no hope for his recovery. On top of everything else, the boy lost his sight.

On May 1st, they took advantage of a moment of lucidity to administer the Holy Viaticum; and on the 4th he received Extreme Unction. His parents realized that the only remedy lay in the Divine omnipotence and goodness, and in the intercession of the Most Holy Virgin to whom so many prodigies are owed. Confiding their son into her care, they had placed a Miraculous Medal around his neck soon after the accident and started a novena in honor of the Mother of God.

On the third day of the novena, about 10 o'clock in the morning, the sick boy suddenly asked if the medal around his neck was blessed. The mother answered yes, considering the question an effect of his delirium. The boy then kissed the medal and sat up in bed. From the time of the fall until that moment he had lain in bed unable to move and had lost all feeling in his legs. He then announced: "They say I am well and that I should get up."

Imagine the surprise of those in the room. The mother called her daughters who were with an older girl, but seeing that the boy insisted that he had been cured, they asked their mother to let him get out of bed. He did so and pointing to a statue in the room representing the medal said: "That was the Mother who cured me!"

From that moment on, the boy was well and continues to be so with his mental faculties even better than before. Commentaries are superfluous. Glory to God and to her who thus rewards the confidence of her devotees! The parents and the cured boy will always remember the gratitude they owe Our Lady and will never cease making it known!

The cure of a girl from Jauchelette, Belgium (1836)

On November 9, 1835, Rosalie Ducas from Jauchelette, near Jodoigne, suddenly lost her sight. She was only four and a half years old, in perfect health with no signs of illness. Any light or breeze disturbed her to the point of having to cover her face with a cloth folded in four. The pains the child suffered day and night caused everyone much grief. Her mother fell ill from affliction.

At this point, a pious person brought a blessed Miraculous Medal. The mother took it and started a novena. On June 11, 1836 at about 6 o'clock in the evening, she put another medal around the girl's neck. By midnight the girl had stopped complaining. On the fourth and fifth day of the novena, her eyes opened. The parents redoubled their supplications to the Most Holy Virgin. On the ninth day in the afternoon, the girl regained her sight completely, to the great surprise of the neighbors and all those who witnessed the event.

The parish priest of Jodoigne-la-Soveraine, who had given the medal to the family, went to see the girl who lived only a mile and a half away, and testified that she had recovered her sight completely. No pain whatsoever was left. These facts are known by everyone and attest to the honor we owe to the Virgin Mary.

The cure of a young girl in Kraków, Poland (1837)

Extract from a letter from Countess Lubinska:

March 12, 1837

Last December 20, I took a girl on as a servant who greatly interested me for her good qualities. She had been in my household only a few days when she started to have very acute headaches. The medicines administered were useless; the attending doctor put her on a diet declaring that the headaches were the result of a liquid that habitually came from her ears. This put her life at risk, or at least her sanity. This opinion seemed to be confirmed by the fact that she needed to walk quickly or bend over forcing her head backward to alleviate the pains. She was compelled to do so many times during the illness. Her continued suffering led her to follow the doctor's advice of undergoing an operation. I trembled at the idea and instructed the sick girl to ask if a delay of ten days would have disastrous consequences. The doctor said it would not and so I stopped all medication and applied a Miraculous Medal. This was Saturday, a day on which the sick girl fasted rigorously in thanksgiving to the Most Holy Virgin who had already miraculously saved her from a deadly typhoid fever. After this cure, her mother had consecrated her daughter to Our Lady, and because of this the girl had great confidence in the Virgin Mary. Some hours after having given her the medal, I heard she had said to one of her friends that she preferred the medal to two thousand francs. It is interesting to note that this pious girl was extremely poor.

To make the miracle more outstanding, God wanted her sufferings to double in intensity that day. And in spite of her patience and resignation, she feared she would not be able to bear the suffering. Knowing the intensity of her Faith and confidence, I deemed it unnecessary to tell her about the happy effects of the medal that I was giving her. When she received it, she made a deliberate Sign of the Cross, repeated the invocation and fell asleep amidst her intolerable sufferings. Upon awakening she was completely cured and since then has not felt any more pains or effects of the sickness.

The cured girl, full of sentiments of humility and lively gratitude, wants to consecrate her life to God by embracing the religious life.

Blessed be God and the Immaculate Mary. And let us make good use of such great mercies!

The Virgin protects a boy in Paris (1837)

Mrs. Rémond, who lives at 70 Mouffetard Street, was holding her twenty-two-month-old son next to an open window on the second floor. Suddenly, she fainted, fell backwards and the baby fell out the window. Normally, he should have been crushed, but that is not what happened.

Ever since his devout parents had heard a pastoral letter from the Archbishop, on the occasion of the consecration of Our Lady of Loreto Church, in which he recommended the faithful to wear a Miraculous Medal, they had placed one around the boy's neck. And Mary Immaculate rewarded this act of piety.

They picked up the poor child, examined him and could not find the slightest bruise. Since the state of the mother needed attention, because she was a few months pregnant and had not yet regained consciousness, they called the doctor. Upon arrival, the doctor also examined the child and could only conclude that a miracle had occurred. However, to be sure, they applied some leeches and a poultice to one knee where the child seemed to feel pain. Although the child had just eaten before his terrible fall, he did not even vomit. He even immediately began to eat sweets they offered him.

Everyone exclaimed that it was a miracle, and the innocent one seemed to do the same by kissing the medal and pressing it constantly to his lips. He does this especially when anyone speaks to him of the fall. I myself observed this pious act when his father presented him to me on June 25, 1837. The mother had no further incident. She is well and never ceases thanking Mary Immaculate for the twofold protection She granted her through the intercession of the medal.

Cures and protection against floods in China (1838)

In a letter dated July 1838, Bishop Rameaux, Vicar Apostolic of the provinces of Kiang-Si and Tche-Kiang sent us the invocation of the medal translated into Chinese. He also related how the Christians in China had a great

devotion to the prayer and never recited a Hail Mary without adding this prayer.
He also said that Bishop de Bézy, Vicar Apostolic of Hu-Kuang and Father Per-
boyre, an apostolic missionary, had some facts of special protection to relate to us.
In fact, some months later, we received the report we will now reproduce here.

— In the province of Hu-Kuang, a Christian, who had been suffering from a horrible fever accompanied by delirium for two months,
had been treated by three doctors and none of the medicine had had
any effect. Being close to death, he called me to administer the sacraments. I gave him the Holy Viaticum and postponed Extreme Unction
because I judged it to be more convenient. I gave him the medal and
advised him to start a novena, assuring him that, if it were for the good
of his soul, he would be cured.

On the seventh day of the novena, the fever left him and he was
immediately made whole. On the ninth day he came to me saying he was
perfectly healthy. I told him to thank the Virgin Mary by praying the
rosary with his friends. However, the man, worried about the business
affairs that his sickness had obliged him to interrupt, forgot to accomplish
what I had suggested. Five days later he had a relapse. This made him
remorseful about not having followed through with my suggestion and
asked for the sacraments once again while re-starting a novena.

The sickness worsened by the day, but I still had great confidence
in Mary the Immaculate and assured him he would be cured before
the end of the novena. Nor was I disappointed. The sick man was
completely cured to the great astonishment of all the Christians. This
time his gratitude was real and the fever did not return.

— In a village in the same province called Tien-Men, the Christians, who numbered some 200, are noted for their piety and for their
great devotion to the Most Holy Virgin. Floods that had lasted eight years
had brought the greatest misery upon them. Seeing the floods occurring
once again, they had recourse to Our Blessed Mother through her
medal. Immediately the waters receded without ruining the lands of the
Christians, although they had caused great damage to those of the pagans.
Seeing this, our Christians acknowledged the protection of Mary and

gave thanks to her for the abundance of their harvest.

Father Perboyre told the next story on August 10, 1839. It is interesting to mention that this missionary was taken prisoner one month later out of hatred for religion. He confessed the Faith generously for a whole year amidst horrible tortures and then had the joy of receiving the martyr's palm on September 11, 1840.

—While I was on mission in the Christian community of Honan in November 1837, the Christians there presented a woman to me who had been suffering from mental confusion for eight months. They added that she ardently desired to make her confession to me even though she was incapable of doing so and implored me not to deny her this consolation that she had so much at heart.

Her unfortunate state really made the exercise of my ministry appear futile. But I heard her confession out of compassion and as she departed I gave her a Miraculous Medal so she would be under the protection of the Virgin. She did not understand the value of this holy remedy, but she soon recognized its virtue as she started to get better. Her progress was such that she was another person after four or five days. Her mental confusion, her worries that had caused her mortal anguish—in which I had noticed a diabolical influence—gave way to common sense, tranquility and happiness.

She went to confession once again and received Holy Communion with fervor and great satisfaction. This further act of goodness on the part of the Mother of Mercies does not surprise us, because her goodness is manifest everywhere. However, I am sure it will give you great joy to once again be able to render her thanks. This is why I bring this prodigy to your attention.

The exorcism of a pagan in Macau (1841)

Letter from a missionary in Macau dated August 25, 1841.

A widow who had been brought up as a pagan had only one son. One day she saw him come under the power of the devil, in other words, possessed. Everyone fled from him as he wandered through the fields making fearful cries. If someone dared to grab him, the boy would immediately throw the person to the ground.

The poor mother was full of pain and sorrow, but Divine Providence had pity on this unfortunate family. One day the boy was more tormented than ever, not knowing where he went and brutally repelling all who drew near. In his wanderings he came upon a Christian, who animated by a lively faith and seeing that the devil tyrannically mistreated the unfortunate boy, told those who were close by to leave. He said that only he was able to calm him down, hold him and return him to his mother. This manner of speaking surprised the pagans. They warned him of the danger, but let him get on with it.

This Christian carried a Miraculous Medal and took it into his hand. Drawing near to the possessed boy, he showed it to him, ordering the devil to leave him alone and depart, which happened immediately. The boy, seeing the Christian with the medal, threw himself to the ground before this image without knowing what it was. The pagans, who had watched him from afar, were astounded. The Christian then said to him that he should rise and follow him. He continued to hold the medal in evidence, which was like a talisman to the young idolater. In this manner he brought him to his mother's house.

As soon as the boy saw her he said: "Do not cry, I am free. The devil left as soon as he saw this medal." Imagine the joy of the mother upon hearing these words. She did not know whether or not she was dreaming.

The Christian certified the truth of what the boy was saying and told her what had happened. He added that her son would be free forever as long as he renounced the idols and became a Christian. The boy sincerely promised to do so and both of them began removing the false idols from a sort of altar where they were kept. Then the Christian, confident they would be faithful to their promises as soon as they had been instructed in the Faith, took his leave. He was thanked profusely by the mother and the son for the great service he had rendered to them!

The protection of Mary in Texas (1841)

From a letter written by Bishop Odin, Vicar Apostolic of Texas:

April 11, 1841

Once I had the occasion to see, in the town of Nacogdoches, how much Mary Immaculate deigns to hear those who place all their confidence in her. A lady from Maryland was given a Miraculous Medal by her confessor as she departed from her home state to go to live in Texas. As he gave it to her, he recommended she always pray: "O Mary conceived without sin, etc." and told her that this good Mother would not permit her to die without receiving the sacraments.

She was faithful to his advice. Having been bedridden for four years, many times her friends thought her last moment had come. However, her confidence in Mary Immaculate always made her hope she would have the joy of receiving the sacraments before departing this life. As soon as she heard of our arrival, she immediately sent us a message. She received the Holy Viaticum and Extreme Unction and died some days later full of gratitude to her Heavenly benefactress.

The conversion of a captain in the Austrian army (1860)

Excerpt of a letter from the Mother Superior of the Daughters of Charity of the hospital of Gratz in Austria:

After the war in Italy, a Polish regiment was passing through Gratz. The commanding officer, a captain, began vomiting blood and was obliged to be hospitalized. While in the hospital, he was taken care of by the Daughters of Charity. Their dedicated treatment did not check the advance of the illness and the sick man was in danger.

Although very courteous and grateful towards those who treated him, he showed a bad disposition if religion was mentioned and asked not to be visited by the chaplain of the regiment. Hearing this, the hospital chaplain dared not even present himself. They tried not to annoy him, because the worst upset could provoke a mortal vomit.

One night, a nun who kept watch over him, inadvertently left a book about graces obtained through devotion to the Holy Virgin near his bedside. The sick man picked the book up and read some of the stories. When another nun came, he showed her one of the stories and raising his hand to his head in a significant gesture said: "Look, Sister, read this absurdity. I do not understand how books like this can be written. If you do not mind, take this away."

In vain they tried to entertain him and to interest him in the state of his soul. He was closed to everything. After a few days one of the nuns risked offering him a medal of the Virgin suspended from a cord so he could wear it. Out of politeness, he did not refuse, but left it where the nun had placed it. His military assistant, although a good Christian, did not dare suggest he receive the sacraments. In spite of his hope that he would soon leave the hospital, the fever increased by the day, leading him rapidly towards death.

The nuns were greatly afflicted with the state of his health, especially over his spiritual condition and decided to make one last effort to save his soul. They decided to write to the Holy Virgin thus: "Most Holy Mother, grant that this man accept your medal, prepare him to receive the sacraments and assist him at the hour of his death. O Mary conceived without sin, forgive our temerity in placing this note in the hands of your statue, where it will remain until you deign to hear our humble supplication." And this is what they did.

As the hospital's head doctor left the room of the sick man, he said to the nun: "The captain will die without receiving the last rites!" "Ah! The Most Holy Virgin will soon take care of that!" she replied.

Three or four days passed, then one morning the sick man called the nun. "Please hang the medal around my neck," he said. In the afternoon he called her again: "I ask you to call my regiment's chaplain. I want to go to confession and tomorrow I would like to receive Communion and Extreme Unction." The priest came immediately. The confession was a long one and, on the following day, after having celebrated Mass on the altar dedicated to the Immaculate Conception, he gave him the Holy

Viaticum and Extreme Unction. The dying man's devotion edified everyone. He devotedly kept his medal, which he kissed many times. Some days later he gave his soul to God having been saved, as we hope, through the intercession of Mary conceived without sin.

The conversion of a sick Protestant in New Orleans, Louisiana (1865)

In the hospital of the Daughters of Charity in New Orleans, a nun tried to instruct a Protestant in the truths of the Faith and to dispose him to receive Baptism. However, he did not want to speak about the subject. One day she showed him a Miraculous Medal and explained its origin to him. He seemed to pay attention, but when she offered it to him, he became annoyed and snapped angrily: "Take that away, this Virgin is just an ordinary woman." "I will leave it on the table," the nun replied, "I am certain that you will think about what I said." He did not answer her, but, in order not to see the medal, he placed his bible on top of it.

Every day the nun, with the pretext of cleaning the table, made sure the medal was still there. Days passed and the sickness became increasingly worse. One night when he was suffering acutely, he saw a marvelous light around his bed, while the rest of the room was in total darkness. Surprised, he struggled to get up in spite of his frailty and turned up the flame in the gas lamp to see if he could discover what this strange light was. He could find nothing and returned to his bed. Moments later he noticed that the light came from the medal.

He then took it into his hands and kept it there the rest of the night. As soon as the nun's rising bell rang at 4 o'clock in the morning, he called the nurse and asked him to tell the nun that he wanted to be baptized. They immediately advised the chaplain who exclaimed, "But, that's impossible!" He had spoken with the sick man many times and knew how he felt about the matter. Nonetheless, he went to him and found him perfectly disposed and receptive to him. He baptized him and gave him the sacraments, and a little while later the sick man died, praising God and the Holy Virgin for the graces he had received.

The cure and conversion of a young Protestant lady in Buffalo, New York (1866)

A Protestant girl, some twenty years old, came to the hospital covered with the most repugnant scabs which the doctors had said were incurable. The nun, who cared for her wounds, one day told her that the Most Holy Virgin had the power to cure her and that, if she wanted to wear the medal and ask for a cure, she would obtain it. The poor girl, knowing the doctors had given up, answered roughly: "I do not believe in your Holy Virgin, nor do I want a medal." "Very well then," the nun answered, "in that case, keep your wounds."

Some days later, she asked for the medal and placed it around her neck, and prepared to be baptized. Shortly thereafter she left the hospital in perfect health to the great astonishment of the doctors who had been unanimous in considering her sickness incurable.

The conversion of a person in Lima, Peru (1876)

Letter from a Sister of Charity in Lima, Peru:

For a long time Mr. N. suffered from hypertrophy cardiomyopathy. The doctors had done all they could and had decided nothing more could be done. They advised the family so the sick man could arrange his affairs. This was indeed a sad piece of news to give to any head of a family, but most especially to one who had no faith.

In vain his relatives and friends discreetly mentioned the idea of receiving the sacraments, but he did not want to listen. A priest, a friend of the family, thought he was obliged to at least try; but he was badly received. Anything to do with religion exasperated the sick man. He blasphemed continuously and did not spare the Most Holy Virgin.

One day someone mentioned the conversion of a certain individual from Lima in the presence of the sick man's relatives who expressed the desire to use the same means for their dear sick relative. "It is simple," he answered, "ask Sister M. from the Hospital of Santa Ana, who gave a medal to the other person, to give you one also. She will not refuse."

One of the sick man's nephews looked for the nun and brought back the precious treasure. One of his nieces offered it to their sick uncle: "Mummy," she said "sends you this medal and asks you to wear it." "Well, I will do it, since your mother sent it. But this does not mean I will go to confession."

Things were tranquil that night and the next day he asked one of his nephews: "Eulógio, what preparations are necessary when undertaking a long journey?" His nephew thought he was dreaming hearing his uncle speak thus and asked what journey he was speaking about. "I want to speak about the journey to eternity," the sick man answered. Satisfied at the change, the boy answered that the best preparation was to put one's conscience in order by making a good confession. "Very well, I will do as you say. Go find a priest for me."

The priest arrived quickly and, after having heard the dying man's confession, went to get the Holy Viaticum. All present were moved at seeing the sick man, almost in his death throes, wanting to receive on his knees, supported by his children, that God Who had just forgiven the sins of his whole life. Moments later, he blessed his children, gave them some last advice and died with sentiments of faith as lively as had been the hardness of his impiety. His family was full of gratitude for having received such a special favor, which redounded to the glory of the Immaculate Mary.

To you, dear reader

We hope these marvelous stories may also help you, dear reader!

The Miraculous Medal continues to multiply its prodigies even today. We know of countless other impressive stories of conversions, graces of moral regeneration, cures of attachment to vices, and infallible protection against the action of the devil. There are innumerable accounts of cures and relief procured in every kind of illness, as well as assistance to expectant mothers and of astounding protection against assault, robbery, kidnapping, accidents and other dangers. And who can count those who have found employment and resolved financial difficulties by means of this devotion? Even in our days, so lacking in true Faith, the facts that take place never cease to surprise and edify us.

When she revealed the Miraculous Medal, Our Lady clearly promised that "everyone who wears it, when it is blessed, will receive great graces, especially if they wear it around their neck." She did not put restrictive conditions, she said "everyone." And then completed the phrase with: "The graces will be abundant to those who use it with confidence."

We all need great graces, especially in these difficult and critical times. Let us turn to the Virgin Mother of God in all our needs and concerns, and ask her with a childlike confidence to answer our prayers.

Dear reader, are you not also in need of a particular grace? Or maybe someone in your family is in need of one, or one of your friends? It was for people like you that the Virgin, the best of all mothers, in her unfathomable mercy, gave us the Miraculous Medal.

It is a providential helping hand from Heaven.

—*America Needs Fatima*

SOURCES

Books

Aladel, Jean-Marie, C.M. *La Médaille Miraculeuse—Origine, Histoire, Diffusion, Résultats*, Édition revue et augmentée. Paris: Pillet et Dumoulin, 1881.

Corrêa de Oliveira, Plinio. *Revolução e Contra-Revolução*, Second Portuguese Edition. São Paulo: Diário das Leis, 1982.

Crapez, Edmond, C.M. *La Venerabile Caterina Labouré Figlia della Carità di San Vincenzo de Paoli*. Rome: Desclée & Cie., 1911.

Crapez, Edmond, C.M. *Le Message du Coeur de Marie à Sainte Catherine Labouré*. Paris: Spes, 1947.

d'Azeredo Teixeira d'Aguilar, Francisco. *A Medalha Miraculosa—sua origem, história, diffusão e resultados* or *Nossa Senhora das Graças, e os Actos da sua Misericórdia*. Porto: Imprensa Commercial, 1884.

de la Franquerie, Marquess. *La Vierge Marie dans l'Histoire de France*. Fontenay-le Comte: Imprimerie Lussaud Frères, 1939.

de Montfort, Louis-Marie Grignion. *Traité de la vraie dévotion à la Sainte Vierge*, Eleventh Canadian Edition. Québec: Librairie Montfortaine, 1946.

Goubert, Joseph and Chanoine L. Cristiani. *Apparitions et Messages de la Sainte Vierge de 1830 à nos jours*. Paris: Éditions du Vieux Colombier, 1952.

Lanquetin, Albert. *Catherine Labouré—La sainte de Reuilly*. Paris: Éditions S.O.S., 1976.

Laurentin, René. *Vie authentique de Catherine Labouré*. Paris: Desclée De Brouwer, 1980.

Laurentin, René and P. Roche, C.M. *Catherine Labouré et la Medaille Miraculeuse — Documents Authentiques*. Paris: Lethielleux, 1976.

Laurentin, René. *Catherine Labouré et la Medaille Miraculeuse—Procès de Catherine*. Paris: Lethielleux, 1979.

Louis-Lefèbvre, Marie-Thérèse. *Le silence de Catherine Labouré*, Second Edition. Bruges: Desclée De Brouwer, 1955.

Machado, Henrique, C.M. *A Medalha Milagrosa, sua história, simbolismo e lições*. Porto: Tipografia Fonseca, 1930.

Molaine, Pierre. *L'itinéraire de la Vierge Marie*. Paris: Éditions Corrêa, 1953.

Rebut, Roger Rebut. *Les Messages de la Vierge Marie*. Paris: Librairie Pierre Tequi

- Éditeur Religieux, 1968.

Yver, Colette. *La vie secrète de Catherine Labouré*. Paris: Spes, 1935.

Marín, Hilario, S.J., ed. *Documentos Marianos—Doctrina Pontificia IV*. Madrid: Biblioteca de Autores Cristianos, 1954.

La Sainte du Silence et le Message de Notre-Dame. Paris: 1968.

Articles

Crapez, Edmond, C.M. "La dévotion mariale chez Saint Vincent de Paul et les Lazaristes ou Prêtres de la Mission." *Maria—Études sur la Sainte Vierge*, vol. III, pp. 95-118. Paris: Beauchesne et ses Fils, 1954.

Gouveia, José Francisco. "A Medalha Milagrosa conserva ainda sua atualidade?" *Catolicismo*, no. 445, January 1988.

Machado, Antônio Augusto Borelli, "Santa Catarina Labouré—A noviça que viu Nossa Senhora." *Catolicismo*, no. 312, December 1976.

Machado, Antônio Augusto Borelli. "Predições de Nossa Senhora a Santa Catarina Labouré." *Catolicismo*, no. 359, November 1980.

Machado, Antônio Augusto Borelli. "Intransigência dos Santos: fidelidade inarredável à sua missão—A firmeza inquebrantável de Santa Catarina Labouré na defesa do verdadeiro simbolismo da Medalha Milagrosa." *Catolicismo*, no. 515, November 1993.

Rábanos, Ricardo, C.M. "La Inmaculada de la Medalla Milagrosa." *Estudios Marianos*, pp. 409-427. Madrid: 1955.

Dictionary Entries

Baudot, J., O.S.B. Entry "Cathérine Labouré." In *Dictionnaire Practique des Connaissances Religieuses*, vol. I. Paris: Letouzey et Ané, 1925.

Bricout, J. Entry "Medaille Miraculeuse." In *Dictionnaire Practique des Connaissances Religieuses*, vol. IV. Paris: Letouzey et Ané, 1926.

Bugninin, Annibale. Entry "Medaglia Miracolosa." In *Enciclopedia Cattolica*, vol. VIII. Città del Vaticano: 1952.

Laurentin, René. Entry "Apparizioni." In *Nuovo Dizionario di Mariologia*. Edited by Stefano de Fiores and Salvatore Meo, Second Edition. Milan: Edizioni Paoline, 1986.